ACCEPTING THE MARK OF THE BEAST

The Final Test of Man's Allegiance to God

KAREN P. PHILLIPS, MDiv.

EQUIP

PRESS

ACCEPTING THE MARK OF THE BEAST

Copyright © 2020 Karen P. Phillips, MDiv.

Published by Equip Press, Colorado Springs, CO

First Edition: 2021
Accepting the Mark of the Beast / Karen P. Phillips, MDiv.
Paperback ISBN: 978-1-951304-60-7
eBook ISBN: 978-1-951304-61-4

EQUIP
PRESS

Dedication

This book is dedicated to my LORD and Savior, Jesus Christ, who gave me this book many years ago.

Table of Contents

Introduction

There have been many great writers of Bible Prophecy—Tim LaHaye, Dr. David Jeremiah, Rev. Ernest Angley, Dr. Ed Hinson, Jonathan Cahn, and Perry Stone, just to name a few. I have read many of their books and respect their attention to biblical integrity and academic scholarship. However, I have never read about the mark of the beast as it relates to prophecy—more specifically, one's acceptance of the mark. None of us really know what it is or how it will come about. The hows, whys, whens, whats, and wheres are not important. The only important thing is that the mark of the beast is real and will come to pass. Even more startling is that many people, even those we least expect, will take it.

Several years ago, I asked the LORD the following question: Since we know what Scripture tells us about the mark, why would anyone take it in the first place? Time passed and I'd forgotten I asked the question. But when I least expected it, the LORD began to unpack for me in Scripture and through revelation how it would come to pass. Using the fall from the Garden of Eden as the foundation and other scriptural examples, the Lord has shown me clues and insights regarding how the mark of the beast will be presented so that men and women will accept it.

There is a lot that I do not know, but I have put in this book what the Lord has allowed me to share. I believe in the truth contained in Scripture. Although I am very concerned about our culture's direction, I understand that the Lord warned us that these times would come. My greatest desire is that this book will shake us out of our spiritual slumber and wake us up to the danger lurking on the horizon.

Karen P. Phillips, MDiv

CHAPTER ONE

The Mark of the Beast

The Significance of the Mark of the Beast

> [16] *He causes all, both small and great, rich and poor, free and slave, to receive a mark on their right hand or on their foreheads,* [17] *and that no one may buy or sell except one who has the mark or the name of the beast, or the number of his name.* (Rev. 13:16-17, NKJV)

What is a mark? Merriam Webster's Dictionary defines the word "mark" in several ways: (1) something set up to be aimed at; (2) a sign or token; (3) inscription, dot, scar, or any visible trace or impression."[1] The mark of the beast is not like any other mark in existence. We get some marks by accident—like when a child scrapes his or her knee while playing or when we get a paper cut. Some marks we get by choice—for example, when we mark our skin through piercings or tattooing. We do this because we agree with our culture or social group that these things are attractive. They are a source of our identity and are desirable behaviors. The same premise of desirable behavior holds true for the mark of the beast.

Accepting the mark of the beast starts with the perspective of desirability. But the process for acceptance will evolve into something far more sinister. In fact, the mark does not just show our association with a social group or admiration for the marking. It shows that the person has decided to cut all ties with God and has fully placed his or her allegiance, confidence, and loyalty in Satan through the figure that would be known as "the Beast" (i.e., the

---

[1] Merriam Webster's Dictionary and Thesaurus, Definition of "Mark" (Springfield: Merriam-Webster, Incorporated, 2006), 651.

Antichrist). By wearing this mark, the wearer has identified him or herself as under the complete ownership of Satan.

Misplaced Worship

> [13] *"You were in Eden, the garden of God; Every precious stone was your covering: The sardius, topaz, and diamond, Beryl, onyx, and jasper, Sapphire, turquoise, and emerald with Gold. The workmanship of your timbrels and pipes was prepared for you on the day you were created.* [14] *You were the anointed cherub who covers; I established you; You were on the holy mountain of God; You walked back and forth in the midst of fiery stones.* [15]*You were perfect in your ways from the days you were created. Till iniquity was found in you.* [16] *By the abundance of your trading You became filled with violence within, And you sinned; Therefore I cast you as a profane thing Out of the mountain of God: And I destroyed you, O covering cherub, From the midst of the fiery stones.* [17] *Your heart was lifted up because of your beauty. You corrupted your wisdom for the sake of your splendor; I cast you to the ground, I laid you before kings, That they might gaze at you."* (Ezek. 28:13-17, NKJV)

In the passage referenced above, the prophet Ezekiel is speaking about the fall of a specific ruler (referred to as the Prince of Tyre). Most scholars implicitly use this text as a reference to Satan's fall from heaven. This is because in the text, Satan tried to usurp God's authority in heaven and was cast out with a third of his demonic angels. Satan's ultimate goal was revealed in this action—to use persuasion and deception to shift allegiance from God to him. It is this same methodology he would employ in the Garden of Eden. Because it worked successfully there, Satan has continued to use this strategy in all his interactions with humans throughout the generations of man.

But allegiance was not the only focus. Satan wanted to replace God as the subject of worship. "Worship refers to the act or action associated with attributing honor, reverence, or worth to that which is considered divine by religious adherents. Christian worship is often defined as an ascription of worth or honor to the Triune God. Worship is more fully understood as an interrelation between divine action and human response. It is the human response to the self-revelation of God. This includes the following: (1) divine initiation in which God reveals Himself, His purposes, and His will; (2) a spiritual and personal relationship with God through Jesus Christ on the part of the worshipper; and (3) a response by the worshipper of adoration, humility, submission, and obedience to God." [2]

Satan desires worship. This desire to be the subject of mankind's worship has been Satan's chief motivation to use trickery and deception. This trickery has caused people to think that God does not mean what He says (see, Gen. 2:16-17 and Gen. 3:1-4); that God does not want mankind to reach its fullest spiritual potential; and that God hides knowledge, wisdom, and the mysteries of the world from mankind (ref. Gen. 3:5). Using deception and manipulation, Satan causes men and women to think evil of God, making them more susceptible to accept his lies and to follow him. The result of this acceptance of Satan is the rejection of God and God's Word. This rebellion against God is actually a form of worship to Satan. Once this occurs, Satan's goal of turning allegiance from God to him has been accomplished.

Objects of Misplaced Worship – (Idolatry)

> "[2] I am the LORD your God, who brought you out of the land of Egypt, out of the house of bondage. [3] You shall have no other gods before Me. [4] You shall not make for yourself a carved image – any likeness of anything that is in heaven above, or that is in the earth beneath, or that is in the water under the earth; [5] You shall not bow down for them or serve them. For I, the LORD your God, am a jealous God, visiting the iniquity of the fathers upon the children to the third and fourth generations of those who hate Me, [6] but showing mercy to thousands, to those who love Me and keep My commandments."
> (Exod. 20:2-6, NKJV)

The verses above were introduced while the children of Israel were on their journey to the Promised Land. They had been delivered from the bondage of slavery. The LORD reminded them of what He had done for them and who He was as their God. While preparing for their exodus from Egypt and travel to the Promised Land, the LORD performed many miracles for them. Some of them included, but are not limited to, the following: (1) during their escape from Egypt, the LORD arranged it so that the Egyptians gave them possessions so that the Israelites would not leave empty-handed (Exod. 12:35-36); (2) The LORD guided the people on their journey as a pillar of

---

2   Brand, Chad, Charles Draper, and Archie England, "Worship" in *Holman Illustrated Bible Dictionary*, ed. (Nashville: Holman Bible Publishers, 2003), 1896-1687.

a cloud in the daytime and a pillar of fire in the night (Exod. 13:21-22); (3) He allowed them to walk through the Red Sea on dry land, and when they crossed over the other side, He lowered the waters of the sea to destroy the Egyptians (Exod. 14:28-30); (4) He caused manna (a wafer-like substance made of coriander seed with the taste of honey) to fall from heaven (Exod. 16:14-15 &16:31-32); (5) He gave them meat and water when they were hungry (Exod. 16:12-13 & 17:6) ; (6) the LORD used Moses to give the people the instructions of God so that they would know what to do and how to survive in the wilderness (Lev. 1:1-27:34).

Moses, under God's authority, was preparing the Israelites to be an example among the nations. They would illustrate what it meant to be under God's protection and provision. They were to be a light in the world to eventually lead other nations to God. But before any of that could happen, the LORD would use their time in the wilderness to break off the habits and mindsets of their enslavement and introduce them to the instructions and lifestyle habits that would be required of them as a holy nation. The purpose of these commandments was to teach them how to foster a relationship with the LORD God and then begin to develop relationships with others God would connect them to.

The Israelites needed to learn about who God was. How could they follow and have a relationship with someone they did not know? Yes, they had experienced the miracles, but this was about learning about Him. As the prophet, Moses was appointed to guide them in their spiritual relationship with God and give them God's expectations. Very early in their wilderness journey, Moses was summoned by God to go up into Mt. Sinai to receive the instructions (The Ten Commandments) that would govern the people.

The Ten Commandments would be different than anything ever done before. First, they were written by God Himself on the back and front of two large stone tables. Second, they expressed the heart of God and what He wanted the people to know about Him, their relationship with Him, and their relationship with others. Third, they were the work of God. God was the author who decided what should be written on the tablets (Exod. 32:16-17).

The Israelites are like so many of us. When we are confronted with situations we do not understand or that are difficult, we get "spiritual amnesia." We forget everything God had done in the past. Moses had been gone for a while, and the Israelites got worried about his safety. So they reverted to what they had picked up in Egypt.....worshipping idols. They did this by pressuring Aaron, the High Priest, into building a golden calf from the jewelry they had brought from Egypt. The people didn't just build the golden calf, but they woke up the next morning after its creation and offered burnt and peace offerings to worship it (Exod. 32:1-6).

This idol worship was not limited to the Israelites' wilderness experience; it also occurred during the time of Daniel. King Nebuchadnezzar of Babylon built a golden image of himself and required the people to worship it when the instruments were played during a certain time of day. If they did not worship it, they would be thrown into a fiery furnace to their deaths (Dan. 3:1-30).

During the end times, the Antichrist will do the exact same thing that King Nebuchadnezzar did and create an image of himself to compel people to worship it. Idolatry is not limited to worshipping objects but also applies to anyone or anything that takes our time, energy, and focus from worshipping the True God. This diverted worship, in the form of building a physical image, is a direct violation of the commandment not to build, serve, bow down to, or worship an idol (Exod. 20:1-5). The true God's greatness and majesty cannot be contained within the confines of a thing created by man. It limits His glory and fails to encompass the fullness of who He is. God is the Creator. As such, the created thing cannot fully capture the glory of the one that created it. It is a perversion of heavenly order and an attempt to make what is divine common.

The Antichrist and the False Prophet – Agents of Misplaced Worship

13 Then I stood on the sand of the sea. And I saw a beast rising up out of the sea, having seven heads and ten horns, and on his horns ten crowns, and on his heads a blasphemous name. 2 Now the beast which I saw was like a leopard, his feet were like the feet of a bear, and his mouth like the mouth of a lion. The dragon gave him his power, his throne, and great authority. 3 And I saw one of his heads as if it had been mortally wounded, and his deadly wound was healed. And all the world marveled and followed the beast. 4 So they worshiped the dragon who gave authority to the beast; and they worshiped the beast, saying, "Who is like the beast? Who is able to make war with him?" 5 And he was given a mouth speaking great things and blasphemies, and he was given authority to continue for forty-two months (Rev. 13:1-5, NKJV).

11 Then I saw another beast coming up out of the earth, and he had two horns like a lamb and spake like a dragon. 12 And he exercises all the authority of the first beast in his presence, and causes the earth and those that dwell in it to worship the first beast, whose deadly

wound was healed. [13] *He performs great signs, so that he even makes fire come down from heaven on the earth in the sight of men.* [14] *And he deceives those who dwell on the earth by the signs which he was granted to do in the sight of the beast, telling those who dwell on the earth to make an image to the beast who was wounded by the sword and lived.* (Rev. 13:11-14, NKJV)

During the time of the mark of the beast, two figures will rise onto the world stage: The Antichrist and the False Prophet. Both figures will be Satan's agents to guide people into worshipping him. They will serve very distinct roles in the end times drama but will function under the power and authority of Satan himself.

The Antichrist will be a leader in control of most of the world's nations during the end times. He will be able to garner this control with his charismatic personality, ability to communicate in several languages, and uncanny knowledge of world politics and affairs. In a world of chaos, the Antichrist will appear to be the answer to prayer. He will broker a treaty with Israel that will appear to bring peace to that area of the world. However, the façade of being a compassionate, diplomatic, and engaged leader will begin to crumble as the last 3.5 years of the tribulation period comes to pass. Then his true nature and plan of having world domination and worship will come to the surface. This will open the door for the required acceptance of the mark of the beast. He will be able to accomplish this with his partnership with the false prophet.

The False Prophet will point the people of the world to the worship of the Antichrist. As the name implies, he will not operate as a true prophet. The biblical standard for a prophet is one selected by God to hear his voice and communicate His instructions for the people. The prophetic office is an important one because the prophet understands the power of words and is responsible for not releasing prophecy before being authorized to do so by God. While many people have moments of prophetic operation, those who operate in the office of the prophet are responsible for staying before God and making sure of what God wants to be done and said. Not everyone is called to the prophetic office. Those, who are called, must have integrity. They are responsible for expressing God's words, which carries weight with those who hear those words.

The False Prophet will get his instructions from Satan. As such, everything the false prophet says and whatever signs and wonders he performs are for deception and entrapment. Those who believe his lies will follow them to their destructive ending. The False Prophet knows Scripture, and like his progenitor

(Satan), he will use it to distort the truth and use it for his advantage. Because he understands the connection between worship and allegiance, he will use the full spectrum of his satanic powers to bring people into worshipping the Antichrist. This may involve the incorporation of music and anything else in his arsenal to attract followers.

Point to Ponder: The False Prophet is an agent of Satan. As such, he will utilize whatever tools that he can obtain from Satan or that Satan has endowed him with to deceive mankind. Music is an important component in worship. It gets the heart and mind prepared to receive whatever the leader is presenting. Prior to his ejection from heaven for trying to usurp God's authority, Satan was called Lucifer and was in charge of angelic worship. Scripture tells us that while in heaven, Lucifer was anointed, gifted, and beautiful until he became corrupted because of pride. (Referenced from Ezekiel 29:14-17)

In his relationship with the Antichrist (the beast), the False Prophet will work to set up the ultimate merging of church and state. Laws and ordinances will be implemented that will require worship of the Antichrist. As illustrated in the previous section, the creation of a statue was to incite worship. In the end times, the False Prophet will even set up a statue in the Antichrist's image. That tangible object of worship will appeal to people. One of the strengths, but sometimes a weakness, of humans is their need for physical connection. Being able to touch and feel makes something real and accessible. The False Prophet and Antichrist will exploit this need.

The purpose of building the statue is to keep the physical presence of the Antichrist before the people. For those who will be persuaded by all the forces of influence coming together, the statue will draw them to get the mark so they can show their allegiance to him. This will help set the atmosphere for the ultimate worship of the Antichrist as the only acceptable religion in the world and the Antichrist as the only person who can be worshipped as god.

For Christians, it will be a perilous time. They will be seen as enemies of this world system and will be targets for extermination because Christian values are in direct opposition in the world and worship of the Antichrist. For a detailed perspective of what the Bible says about the operation of both the Antichrist and the False Prophet, Table A (listed below) has a side-by-side comparison.

Table A – Comparison between the Antichrist and False Prophet

The Antichrist	Scripture Reference	The False Prophet	Scripture Reference
The Antichrist is described as a beast. This suggests that he has a ferocious, animalistic nature.	Revelation 13:1	The False Prophet will have appear to be Christ-like; but will speak like a dragon (ref. Satan). This means he will be a liar.	Revelation 12:9; Revelation 13:11; John 8:44
Will have control over seven kingdoms and will head up a ten nation confederacy that will have given their power and control over to the Antichrist. Some of the nations that are identified in this group are represented by animals. Leopard: (Germany), Bear (Russia), and Lion (Great Britain).	Revelation 13:1	He will have all of the power of the Antichrist and will direct people to worship Antichrist.	Revelation 13:12
Satan gives the Antichrist his power, authority, and position.	Revelation 13:2	He will use lying wonders and false miracles to deceive people. (Ex. To make fire come from heaven)	Revelation 13:13-14; Genesis 19:24; 1 Kings 18:38; 1 Chronicles 21:26; and 2 Kings 1:10-14
There was a false wonder where a wound was healed. This caused many to wonder about the Antichrist's power and worship the Antichrist and Satan.	Revelation 13:3-4	He causes those on earth to erect an image of the beast	Revelation 13:14; Deuteronomy 5:8-9; Matthew 6:24; Exodus 32:2-5; 1 Timothy 6:13; Acts 17:23-29; Psalm 15:4-8
The Antichrist's power is limited to 42 months or 3 and ½ years.	Revelation 13:5	Through satanic power, the image (statue) of the beast will speak and cause those who do not worship the image to be killed	Revelation 13:15; Exodus 20:5; and Leviticus 26:1
Satan gives the Antichrist the ability for compelling and persuasive oratory. Many of his talks were to blaspheme God, His name, His tabernacle, and those that dwelt in heaven.	Revelation 13:6	The False Prophet will cause all those whose name is not written in the Lamb's Book of Life to receive the mark of the beast on their right hands or foreheads. Without it, the people will not be able to buy and sell.	Revelation 13:16-17
The Antichrist had the power to make war with the saints and to overcome them. Power was given to him over all kindreds, tongues, and nations.	Revelation 13:7		
Those whose names are not written in the Lamb's Book of Life will worship the Antichrist.	Revelation 13:8		

Six: The Magic Number

> ^{17} *and that no one may buy or sell except one who has the mark or the name of the beast, or the number of his name.* ^{18} *Here is the wisdom. Let him that has understanding calculate the number of the beast, for it is a number of a man: His number is 666."* (Rev. 13:17-18, NKJV).

The above quote provides insight into what the mark of the beast could be. It might be the name of the beast or the number of his name. But whatever form the mark takes, it will tie back to the number 666. E.W. Bullinger, in his book, *The Number in Scripture: Its Supernatural Design and Spiritual Significance*, outlines the importance of the number six in the following quote,

> "Six is either 4 plus 2, i.e., man's world (4) with man's enmity to God (2) brought in: or it is 5 plus 1, the grace of God made of none effect by man's addition to it, or perversion, or corruption of it: or it is 7 minus 1, i.e., man's coming short of spiritual perfection. In any case, therefore, it has to do with man. It is the number of imperfection; the human number; the number of MAN as destitute of God, without God, without Christ." [3]

Bullinger's explanation about the number six adds clarity to why the number of the mark of the beast is important. It highlights man's reliance upon his own resources, ingenuity, thoughts, creativity, and failures. In light of these shortcomings, the number six is a celebration of man relying on himself and leaving God completely out of the equation.

Why is the number 666 used specifically? The answer to this lies in what the Lord showed to me several years ago. Satan always tries to imitate whatever God is doing. It is not authentic because it is not God. But Satan can make the substitute appear real. Though it is only an imitation, its appearance is real enough to deceive people.

How does this work? Let's look at the concept of the Trinity. One of the most respected theologians in the field of systematic theology is Wayne Grudem. In his book, *Systematic Theology: An Introduction of Biblical Doctrine*, Grudem defines the concept of the Trinity as follows:

> "It is God eternally existing as three persons, Father, Son, and Holy Spirit, and each person is fully God and there is one God. The word "trinity" is never found in the Bible. The word itself means "triunity" or "three in oneness." [4]

We must understand that each facet of the Trinity is fully God. Each part is perfect and operates in full spiritual perfection. Bullinger tells us again in his book that the number seven signifies "spiritual perfection." [5] So, using

---

[3]   Bullinger, E.W., *The Number in Scripture: Its Supernatural Design and Spiritual Significance* (Grand Rapids: Kregel Publications, 1967), 150.

[4]   Grudem, Wayne, *Systematic Theology: An Introduction to Biblical Doctrine* (Grand Rapids: Zondervan, 1994), 226-227.

[5]   Ibid., 158.

this reasoning, we can think of the Trinity as being the fullness of God's perfection represented in each of its three parts. Each part is perfect on its own as well as part of the whole. We can break it down like this: the first seven represents God (7), the second seven represents Jesus Christ, the Son of God (7), and the third seven represents the Holy Spirit (7). If we could assign a number to represent the perfection of the Trinity, it would be 777.

By converse, we would do the same thing as it applies to Satan and his demonic alliance. Because Satan tries to imitate everything that God does, his version of the Trinity would be a copycat. This is what the number 666 is. It is similar but unlike the Trinity because it is symbolic of the unholy alliance Satan will establish in the last days. 666 would be represented as follows: the first six represents Satan (6); the second six represents the Antichrist (6); and the third six represents the false prophet (6).

They would operate under Satan's power but have their own specific function as it relates to deceiving mankind. Instead of operating in spiritual perfection, they will operate in spiritual darkness and depravity. The number 666 is the visible illustration of the fullness of man's spiritual imperfection and rejection of God. The number is so infamous because it represents its wearer's conscious decision to reject God and give their total allegiance to Satan.

Acceptance of this mark represents the highest point of human vanity! When people start to rely totally on their own ingenuity and forget that God is central to everything, then they are headed down a dangerous road. We must realize that our very existence depends on God's mercy. When He decides to remove the breath from our body, we die. Our possessions are not because of anything we have done. We only have anything because God decided to grant us access. This is generous since God owns everything. Let's see what the Scriptures tell us about God's ownership:

> "Then God saw everything that He had made, and indeed it was very good. So the evening and the morning were the sixth day (Gen. 1:31). Thus the heavens and the earth, and all the host of them, were finished (2:1). And on the seventh day, God ended his work which He had done, and He rested on the seventh day from all His work which He had done (2:2). Then God blessed the seventh day and sanctified it, because in it He rested form all His work which God had created and made (2:3)." (Gen. 1:31-2:3, NKJV)
>
> "The earth is the Lord's and all its fullness. The world and those who dwell therein." (Ps. 24:1, NKJV)

"...for the earth is the Lord's and all its fullness." (1 Cor. 10:26, KJV)

Because we do not own anything, we do not have the right to be arrogant about our possessions. If it was because of our intelligence, talent, or skill that we have jobs, clothes, houses, and possessions, then we would have reason to boast. But since it is only due to God's mercy, we cannot boast or claim that we own anything. God doesn't give us things because He has to. He gives us things because He chooses to share a portion of what He owns with us. When we forget that, we will become slaves to our stuff and are open prey for the enemy.

Seeing Is Believing

[13] He performs great signs, so that he even makes fire come down from heaven on the earth in the sight of men. [14] And he deceives those who dwell on the earth by those signs which he was granted to do in the sight of the beast, telling those who dwell on the earth to make an image to the beast who was wounded by the sword and lived. [15] He was granted power to give breath to the image of the beast, that the image of the beast should both speak and cause as many as would not worship the image of the beast to be killed. (Rev. 13:13-15, NKJV)

One of the greatest gifts God gave to man was the ability to see. With this gift of sight, we can take in the fullness of God's creation. We can see the green leaves of spring transition to the array of burgundy, gold, and brown leaves of fall. We can appreciate the smile of our children and friends. We can enjoy the text of our favorite book. We can see the rain fall and the impact of wind upon trees and bushes. Like with all the senses (hearing, touching, smelling, and tasting), the ability to see allows us to perceive the world around us, make decisions, and respond to the decisions we make.

While the ability to see can be one of our greatest assets, it can (if not used correctly and without the Holy Spirit's guidance) be a trap for us. One example of this can be found in Matthew 5:27-28 (NKJV). Jesus Himself says the following:

[27] You have heard that it was said to those of old, 'You shall not commit adultery.' [28] But I say to you that whoever looks at a woman to lust for her has already committed adultery with her in his heart."

Another example is also found in Matthew 13:14-15 (NKJV):

> "[14] *And in them the prophecy of Isaiah is fulfilled, which says: 'Hearing you will hear and shall not understand, And seeing you will see and not perceive;* [15] *For the hearts of this people have grown dull. Their ears are hard of hearing, And their eyes they have closed, Lest they should see with their eyes and hear with their ears, Lest they should understand with their hearts and turn, So that I should heal them.'"*

Both verses tell us that our ability to see clearly is impacted by the condition of our hearts. If our hearts have not been converted by salvation and under the direction of the Holy Spirit, then our ability to see the world as it is (not just physically, but spiritually) is clouded because our own nature is clouded by sin. Our sin nature causes us to want to satisfy our most deep, evil, and corrupted lusts at any cost. As a result, our ability to perceive spiritual truths is distorted, which allows us to fall prey to deception. This is why when our thoughts are under deception, our physical and spiritual seeing becomes faulty and we adopt the following truths about the things we see and perceive:

- Because I see it, it must be real.
- Because I see it, it must be factual.
- Because I see it, I can believe everything I see.
- Because I see it, then I can trust what I see because *my* eyes do not lie.

So from this viewpoint, it is not out of the realm of reason that someone like the Antichrist can be believed when he comes to power and why some will willingly accept the mark of the beast. In fact, it is inevitable! Revelation 13:8 (NKJV) confirms it by saying:

> *All who dwell on the earth will worship him, whose names have not been written in the Book of Life of the Lamb slain from the foundation of the world.*

CHAPTER TWO

The Landscape of the Mind

The Pathology of the Mind

> [1] *I beseech you therefore, brethren, by the mercies of God, that you present your bodies a living sacrifice, holy, acceptable to God, which is your reasonable service.* [2] *And do not be conformed to this world, but be transformed by the renewing of your mind, that you may prove what is that good and acceptable and perfect will of God.* (Rom. 12:1-2, NKJV)

The human mind is a complex organ. It is the center of our emotions, intellect, will, and actions. The mind works in tandem with the heart to develop a person's character and personality. Because of the mind's power, a person's thoughts will guide their actions.

The transformation of the mind from one that is obedient to God to one that is in enmity with God starts with the information the mind receives. Let us take the example of Adam and Eve from Genesis chapters 1 through 3. God created Adam and Eve in His image and likeness, intending to make them examples of His glory in the earth (ref. Gen. 1:26-27). God gave them dominion over creation (ref. Gen. 1:28-29) and gave Adam the ability to give names to the creatures (ref. Gen. 2:19-20). He only gave Adam one commandment —not to eat from the tree of the knowledge of good and evil, or both Adam and Eve would surely die (ref. Gen. 2:15). The commandment about what they could do and not do was clear.

However, when the serpent approached Eve, it presented a question that piqued her curiosity. She began to process God's commandment in a different way. It was not that she did not understand it or was confused about any of its components. But what changed was how she began to perceive God, herself, and her relationship with God. Eve's understanding of the commandment was affirmed by her ability to respond to the serpent with understanding and being able to dissect it (ref. Gen. 3:2).

The difference in what God said and her interpretation of the commandment altered the commandment in its essence. God only said not to eat from the tree, but nothing about touching it. Her changing of the commandment violated its purity and opened the door for deception to enter. Furthermore, when the serpent lied and said that Eve would not die, this challenged her logic even more. She knew what God had said, and she knew God. But Eve's mind was clouded with the possibility of not dying even though God said otherwise. Additionally, when she was presented with the idea that God was trying to keep wisdom and knowledge from her, she chose to believe the lie even though she knew God would not keep anything good away from her. Now a breach in her mind and animosity in her heart had formed against God. So the thought of eating the fruit God had forbidden became her heart's greatest desire instead of the object of her avoidance.

By nature, humans are logical beings. We process the world around us based on the information we receive about it. Using our reasoning ability, we will take the information we are given, process that information, and direct our behavior based on the information we receive. If we receive godly information and choose to accept and apply that information, we will operate according to God's commandments. Conversely, if we ingest information from ungodly sources, then we will operate in opposition to what Scripture defines as Christ-like behavior, just like Adam and Eve did.

If we fast forward to our society today, our collective psyche is being transformed to accept lifestyles and behavior that decades ago would be scandalous. Behaviors like open sexuality and promiscuity are celebrated on television, books, film, and even in some classrooms. While we choose to have a godly mind, we can also choose to have an ungodly one. It just depends on the information we receive and allow to influence our minds.

For a moment, let us consider what is being portrayed today. It is nothing to see homosexual relationships, adultery, and violence against women and children being played out in living color. Why? Over time and with consistent exposure to these acts, our society has become de-sensitized. As our mindset has changed, we have chosen to accept acts that we know are contrary to godly behavior. Many of us want to be seen as tolerant and accepting, but at what cost? The cost is that the moral climate of our nation and its people is being eroded.

As society continues its cultural shift, Christ-like values are seen as old-fashioned, detrimental, and divisive to the overall good. Society's moral compass has changed. Now, many people's guide for determining right and wrong is based on their own concepts instead of the truth of Scripture. Scripture is clear about how we are to think and the lifestyle we must live to be in right-standing with God. God's standards are always in direct conflict with culture.

No one likes to be painted in a negative light, but Christians are seen as a threat to culture. When people feel threatened, they respond with violence or some other tactic to let the threat know not to mess with them. Because of the perceived threat to worldly behavior, the Christian will be seen as an obstacle to be dealt with because the Christian life is in direct opposition to the "new normal." When that happens, it will open the door for ideas such as the mark of the beast to be introduced.

The Collective Psyche

> [1] *Now the whole earth had one language and one speech.* [2] *And it came to pass, as they journeyed from the east, that they found a plain in the land of Shinar, and they dwelt there.* [3] *Then they said to one another, "Come, let us make bricks and bake them thoroughly." They had brick for stone, and they had asphalt for mortar.* [4] *And they said, "Come let us build ourselves a city, and a tower whose top is in the heavens; let us make a name for ourselves, lest we be scattered abroad over the face of the whole earth."* (Gen. 11:1-7, NKJV)

What does the word "collective psyche" mean? Dictionary.com defines the words separately in the following way: (1) Collective is something that is characteristic of a group of individuals taken together, and (2) psyche is the mental or psychological structure of a person. From these definitions, I wanted to know two things: (1) how can (almost) an entire society be persuaded to think one thing? And (2) what kind of power must one have to achieve such a feat?

For the answers to these questions, one only has to look in the pages of history. We can see example after example where dictators had their countries under absolute control through the tactics of fear, violence, political control, and military might. Some of the most famous examples are Joseph Stalin (Russia), Pol Pot (Vietnam), Idi Amin (Uganda), Saddam Hussein (Iraq), Benito Mussolini (Italy), Hideki Tojo (Japan), and Nicolae Ceausescu (Romania). One of the most infamous examples of absolute evil in the pages of history is Adolf Hitler. With his powerful oratory skill and masterful use of propaganda, Hitler convinced the German people during World War II that the Jewish people were the source of their country's economic and social woes and had to be destroyed.

This ideology was formed in the aftermath of World War I. After the war, Germany's economy was a disaster. There was a huge depression, and Germans were out of work and starving. When Hitler came on the scene, he promised to restore the economy to the pre-WWI status. After he was elected chancellor and eventually Fuhrer, Hitler made Jews the scapegoats for the economy's suffering. Propaganda depicted Jews as dirty, sneaky thieves and sexual deviants.

Furthermore, Hitler blatantly announced that Germany's future success as an Aryan-only nation depended on the destruction and elimination of Jews from European soil. He put laws into place where anyone who had any percentage of Jewish blood could be subject to harsh punishments or deportations to concentration camps. One of his key cabinet leaders, Joseph Goebbels, spent large amounts of money putting out literature to show how inferior Jews were. These images influenced the minds of the German people so that they began to believe these ideas about the Jews were true.

In the book *Inside Hitler's Germany: A Documentary History of Life in the Third Reich*, Benjamin Sax and Dieter Kuntz note two key factors that aided the spread of anti-Semitism:

> (1) "Targeting the population demographics that was hit hardest by the economic turmoil of the time. Those included the middle-class, unemployed salaried workers, young academic talent who have lost all hope of making a living in the future, and administrative workers such as postal workers and the railroad system; and (2) the type and scope of the Nazi Party's propaganda. Selected districts are inundated with propaganda operations consisting of methodically and skillfully prepared written and verbal appeals as well as meetings, all of which, in terms of sheer activity, cannot be matched by any other party or political movement. Carefully organized propaganda headquarters in the individual districts ensure that speakers and topics are in tune

with local conditions and economic circumstances. Propaganda is backed up by SA people who go to the meetings and offer support to the speaker. If necessary, they are a coercive force in that they do not allow anyone to interject or contradict the speaker, which makes it impossible for anyone to make counterarguments."[6]

If we add to this the use of anti-Jewish print literature, posters, magazines, and film, the atmosphere was a fertile breeding ground for turning most of the German populace into willing participants in Hitler's deadly plan of Jewish extermination.

> "Feelings are often sustained by ideas and images. Hopelessness and rejection (feelings of worthlessness and 'not belonging') live on in images – often of some specific scene or scenes of unkindness, brutality, or abuse. These scenes have become a permanent fixture within the mind, radiating negativity and leaving a background of deadly ideas that take over how we think and structure our world.[7]

So if we use this as our example, the question of how a so-called intelligent society could change its mindset into a destructive one is easy. All it takes is for destructive ideas to be introduced repeatedly, persuasively, and with consent over a long period. Eventually, the idea is no longer seen as wrong but as the correct viewpoint.

One may argue that this kind of brainwashing could never happen in North America…right? Wrong. All human beings have the same foundation. However, the framework built around that foundation is different for every individual. The differences are determined by the choices we make about what we allow to shape us. If we focus on gratifying and feeding those things that satisfy our carnal selves (like material possessions or pursuing wealth), then our motivations will be governed by that. We will constantly try to keep those things that satisfy and feed our flesh. By contrast, if our focus is on spiritual things, then the desire to pursue Christ and the things of Christ will grow stronger (see Gal. 5:16-24). We must understand that the ability to alter the mindset of a collective body of people can happen anywhere with anyone whose mind is not renewed with the Spirit of Christ.

---

6   Sax, Benjamin and Dieter Kuntz, *Inside Hitler's Germany: A Documentary History of Life in the Third Reich* (Lexington: D.C. Heath and Company, 1992), 98-100.

7   Willard, Dallas and Don Simpson, *Revolution of Character: Discovering Christ's Pattern for Spiritual Transformation* (Colorado Springs: Nav. Press, 2005), 106.

This destructive behavior of hatred is at the heart of anti-Semitism and will be at the root of acceptance of the mark of the beast. If one can create an atmosphere where prejudices are amplified and divisions are encouraged, then the seeds of hatred can be easily spread.

The Distorted Mind

> [19] *...because what may be known of God is manifest in them, for God has shown it to them.* [20] *For since the creation of the world His invisible attributes are clearly seen, being understood by the things that are made, even His eternal power and Godhead, so that they are without excuse, so that they are without excuse,* [21] *because, although they knew God, they did not glorify Him as God, nor were thankful, but became futile in their thoughts, and their foolish hearts were darkened.* [22] *Professing to be wise, they became fools.* (Rom. 1:19-22, NKJV)

In today's society, most people have a general understanding of the mark of the beast. They may not understand all its nuances or how it works, but they have heard about it or read about it. Yet none of those things mean they believe that it is real. Those who do have some understanding may not actually believe they will encounter it during their lifetime.

The world where the mark of the beast will exist is a much different one from the world we know today. In fact, the issues we face today pale in comparison with the horrors that will exist at that time. The presence of the Holy Spirit will be gone. Godly standards of goodness, morality, and love will be non-existent. Matthew 10:21-23 and Matthew 24:9-10 (NKJV) gives us some insight into how people will interact with one another during this time. The verses read as follows:

> [21] *"Now brother will deliver up brother to death, and a father his child; and children will rise up against parents and cause them to be put to death.* [22] *And you will be hated by all for My name's sake. But he who endures to the end will be saved.* [23] *When they persecute you in this city, flee to another. For assuredly, I say to you, you will not have gone through the cities of Israel before the Son of Man comes."* (Matt. 10:21-23, NKJV)
>
> [9] *"Then they will deliver you up to tribulation and kill you, and you will be hated by all nations for My name's sake.* [10] *And then many*

will be offended, will betray one another, and will hate one another."
(Matt. 24:9-10, NKJV)

In other words, brothers will turn in brothers. Children will turn in parents. Parents will turn in children, and neighbors will turn in neighbors to the authorities. These people will be taken to the authorities because they do not have the mark of the beast. Society will have people brainwashed to the point of believing it is their civic duty and morally correct to turn in their Christian friends and relatives.

The ethical mandates of the Bible will be replaced with a satanic "free for all," where anything and everything one's mind conjures up will be acceptable and acted upon. Anyone who does not fall into line with everyone else will be considered subversive and an enemy of the state. How does society shift to the point of accepting the mark of the beast? How does one support something that is consciously evil? It begins by changing what one's concept of evil is. Webster's Dictionary defines "evil" as something morally reprehensible.[8]

True morality is not determined by human standards but by God's. So whatever God says is unholy or evil, it is so! Satan and his forces must distort what God has said or attempt to remove the evidence of His presence so that the only choice that remains is his. Satan must alter mankind's mindset so that evil is not seen as evil but as good.

In this world turned upside down, the mark of the beast must be seen as not just good but necessary to the continued advancement of society. That is done by attacking four key areas that humans use to reason and make choices: (1) the use of logic; (2) whether something is attractive or has visual appeal; (3) whether something is vital to our everyday living or function; and (4) ease.

Logic

Human beings are thinking beings. We process our world through our senses, experiences, and the context clues we get from our environment. The mark of the beast must make sense to human reasoning. For example, consider national security. With the 911 attacks, the United States recognized for the first time how vulnerable it really is. Muslim terrorists who had been trained in the United States had been able to slip in through airport security and cause the destruction of lives and property in New York (the World Trade

---

8   Merriam-Webster's Dictionary and Thesaurus, 370.

Center) and in other areas around the country. A worldwide centralized security system could have linked up personal history and background from databases from all over the world to decipher the identity and profiles of every individual who passed through airport security. As a result, lives and property could have possibly been saved. This sounds reasonable…. Right?

Attractiveness/Visual Appeal

Our ability to see is one of our most powerful senses. We make a lot of judgments based on what we see. We make assessments about people, their status, character, and what they must be like as people based upon what we see. Some of us dye our hair because we think having colored hair or hair without gray strands makes us more attractive. We wear certain clothes because we think what we wear makes us more appealing.

An added benefit to what we wear is that it might create a sense of community or align us with a particular social group. Fraternities and sororities wear certain colors, Greek letters, and symbols to identify which group a person is affiliated with. Church organizations such as the Masons, Shriners, or Eastern Stars may use certain colors and rituals in their organizations. Our companies, social organizations, and clubs all have things that link our participation to the group. Although church groups, social groups, and Greek letter organizations are different than what is associated with the mark of the beast, the common denominator is to create a sense of belonging. Revelation 13:16 (NKJV) gives us some important insights about the social aspect of the mark:

> [16] *He causes all, both small and great, rich and poor, free and slave,*
> *to receive a mark on their right hand or on their foreheads…"*

The location of the mark is significant as well. We see in the text that it is in two prominent locations: forehead and right hand. The right hand is synonymous with being a place of honor or distinction (see Gen. 48:13-19 and 1 Kgs. 2:19). The forehead is the place where crowns rest and is symbolic of authority (see Matt. 27:29 and Rev. 19:12). Although many assumptions can be made, the fact that most of the society will have the mark will be strong motivation for many. It will create a feeling of being important, being in charge, and being part of something bigger than the individual. This can be especially attractive for someone who does not understand the full meaning of taking the mark and only wants to be a part of a community.

Vital

When something is seen as necessary or vital, we are more prone to take action. With the mark of the beast, the key motivation is that the ability to conduct business does not exist without the mark. Revelation 13:17 (NKJV) tells us the extent of the controls that will be put into place:

> [17] *and that no one may buy or sell except one who has the mark or the name of the beast, or the number of his name."*

Let's look at something as common as going to the grocery store during this time. Most of us wait until the last minute. The staple items have been eaten, and now the canned goods and surplus supplies are getting low. At this time, one will not be able to go to family and friends who have the mark. Why? They will turn you in. Is there someone without the mark that you can trade with? If you go to them or they come to you, you risk exposure. What do you do? These are the types of questions that people without the mark will have to face. For some, the pressures of this new way of living will force them to make hard decisions about whether to accept the mark.

What about holding a job? All of us know that being able to exist depends on having access to making money. We must have money to buy the things we need to survive and function. To do business during this time, companies may be required to sign contracts with the government, promising to comply with whatever stipulations are put into place. Policies may require prospective employees to receive the mark prior to employment or for existing employees to obtain the mark by a certain deadline to retain their employment.

Preparing employees for this type of strategy may take the form of required training programs. I have worked for companies that required employees to take mandatory annual training. In some instances, email notifications are sent to leadership about employees in danger of missing the deadline. This pressures the employee to take their training so their supervisor will not have to address the matter again. If the training is still not taken by the deadline, disciplinary action is taken, documented, and put into the employee's personnel file. This strategy could be implemented to mentally pressure employees to take the mark to keep their jobs and livelihoods. Some living during this time will believe they can take the mark and then have a "do-over" or have it removed. **There are no second chances with the mark of the beast**. Once the mark is taken, the choice has been made (see Rev. 14:9-12).

Ease

Many humans are lazy by nature—not in the sense of being slothful, but we prefer to do things that will cause us to expend minimal effort. For example, carrying cash or personal checks has given way to the convenience of ATMs and credit cards. Now, because of identity theft and credit card hacking, new solutions offer a way to conveniently and securely integrate financial and other information.

What would be more convenient than downloading everything associated with a person *on* the person? Information such as medical history, prescribed medications, creditworthiness, job history, criminal background, friend and familial information, housing history, education, vocational background, purchasing history, personal preferences, and other demographic information could be accessed in a chip or other small device implanted into the skin. This could be a key selling point for accepting the mark of the beast. One would not have to worry about carrying anything because everything a person needs would be embedded into them—on the right hand or the forehead.

True Knowledge Only Comes from God

> [1] *My son, if thou wilt receive my words, And treasure my commands within you.* [2] *So that you incline your ear to wisdom, And apply your heart to understanding.* [3] *Yes, if you cry out for discernment. And lift up your voice for understanding.* [4] *If you seek her as silver, And search for her as for hidden treasures.* [5] *Then you will understand the fear of the Lord, And find the knowledge of God."* (Prov. 2:1-6, NKJV)
>
> *"My people are destroyed for lack of knowledge. Because you have rejected knowledge, I will also reject you from being priest for Me. Because you have forgotten the law of your God. I also will forget your children."* (Hosea 4:6, NKJV)

Both Bible verses above speak of the need for knowledge. This is not the knowledge that is devised by human imagination or thought but the knowledge one can only get from the source of all knowledge—God, the Eternal One. He formed the world before anything ever existed and is the only one from whom the depths of all knowledge comes. This knowledge is eternal and unending. This repository of knowledge comes through revelation from the Holy Spirit and from the pages of the Holy Bible. Great care has been taken to preserve and transcribe from the original oral traditions everything God has said either directly or through human vessels preserved in the Bible.

We have many Bible translations that range from the Wycliffe Bible and King James Version to versions written in everyday language, such as the North American Standard, Modern English Version, or The Message Bibles. With so many varieties, we have no reason not to read it. Additionally, if we agree that the Bible is the sole authority of life and living, then why are people not reading it? Some of the excuses I hear are as follows:

- I don't have time.
- I don't own a version that I can read.
- I don't find the Bible interesting.
- I can just get what I need out of the Bible when I go to church on Sunday.
- It is too hard to read.
- I cannot believe what is in the Bible because too many people have translated it.

Let's look at reading the Bible from another perspective. For example, suppose a million dollars was placed inside the Bible and placed on a table in the middle of an open field just to see if someone would open it. If no one told them what was inside, I wonder how many people would go out and open it and find the million dollars. If any of the above responses are an indication of people's perspective on reading the Bible, then the million dollars would remain undiscovered for a long time.

The Bible is a treasure trove of information. Contained within its pages are insights about how God thinks, promises He has made, instructions for lifestyle and living, words of encouragement and strength, and revelation to prepare for the future. It is terrifying to think that because many people do not or refuse to read the Bible, they will be ill-prepared or completely unaware of the Lord's warnings. But the Lord does not just give knowledge, but He combines it with understanding. He wants us not just to know His Word but to understand why He does what He does.

Unfortunately, our lack of desire to read the Bible is the very thing Satan revels in. Satan knows Scripture. The indictment is that many of us do not know it very well. Our ignorance provides Satan with the perfect opening to present us with deception that will lead to destruction. If you don't believe that can happen, just remember Adam and Eve in the Garden of Eden. The twisting of God's Word and disobedience to that Word led Adam and Eve to be evicted from Eden, and it introduced the curse of sin to humankind. It happened once, and it will happen again!

Don't Believe the Hype

> [18] *"What profit is the image, that its maker should carve it, The molded image, a teacher of lies, That the maker of its mold should trust in it, To make mute idols?* [19] *Woe to him who says to wood, Awake! To silent stone, Arise! It shall teach! Behold, it is overlaid with gold and silver. Yet in it there is no breath at all."* (Hab. 2:18-19, NKJV)
>
> [11]*"Then I saw another beast coming up out of the earth, and he had two horns like a lamb and spake like a dragon.* [12] *And he exercises all the authority of the first beast in his presence, and causes the earth and those that dwell in it to worship the first beast, whose deadly wound was healed.* [13] *He performs great signs, so that he even makes fire come down from heaven on the earth in the sight of men.* [14] *And he deceives those who dwell on the earth by the signs which he was granted to do in the sight of the beast, telling those who dwell on the earth to make an image to the beast who was wounded by the sword and lived.* [15] *He was granted power to give breath to the image of the beast, that the image of the beast should both speak and cause as many as would not worship the image of the beast to be killed."* (Rev. 13:11-15, NKJV)

Habakkuk was one of the minor prophets of the Old Testament. In his writings, he cries out to God for His lack of response regarding the violence in the land. Habakkuk decrees that God has raised up enemies against Israel so they would be driven to repentance and turn back to God. Additionally, he issues a series of warnings to the unrighteous so they will be aware of the penalties God will levy against them for their disobedience. Sandwiched in the text is a warning to those who make graven images and worship them. The prophet reminds the reader that these objects are crafted by man's hands and have no life.

If we contrast these verses with Revelation 13:11-15, we see a key point. Habakkuk reminds us that graven images are not items to worship. But in Revelation 13:15, we see a statue that speaks and invokes action to cause people to worship the image of the beast. Because of this seemingly supernatural occurrence, many will be deceived. It will appear that because it is so miraculous, it had to be God's doing. Why? It defies human logic.

Because people realize that objects do not speak, those who witness this statue speaking will be amazed. They will be in such awe that they will not care about the source of the occurrence. As a result, many will flock to and worship Satan's image, to their destruction.

This is an important key, and I put it in bold text so that no one will miss this:

In the beginning stages, the mark of the beast will be presented as *optional* worship to ease people into the process. Even though the statue speaks by satanic power, amazement will drive people to worship it. In addition, people will worship the image because they will believe the lie that God does not want people to be their best selves and is keeping mankind from reaching a higher spiritual level.

People will react the same way Adam and Eve did in the Garden of Eden. They will want what they perceive is being held back from them and will accept the mark of the beast. As time progresses and when the results desired are not being achieved, then force will be used to compel people to take the mark. Ultimately, those who do not worship the image of the beast by taking the mark will be killed (see Rev. 15:15).

CHAPTER THREE

Inhibitions Unleashed!

The Impact Is Instant!

> ⁶*So when the woman saw that the tree was good for food, that it was*
> *pleasant to the eyes, and a tree desirable to make one wise, she took of*
> *its fruit and ate. She also gave to her husband with her, and he ate.*
> ⁷*Then the eyes of both of them were opened, and they knew that they*
> *were naked; and they sewed fig leaves together and made themselves,*
> *coverings.* (Gen. 3:6-7, NKJV)

Although we do not know exactly how the mark of the beast will be administered, how it will look, or when it will be implemented, Scripture does give us some insight into how it will impact those who accept it. As we previously learned, there are strong correlations between eating the fruit in the Garden of Eden and accepting the mark of the beast. Both demonstrate man's outright rejection of God's commandments. In Genesis, the command was not to eat of the fruit of the Tree of Knowledge of Good and Evil.

Regarding the mark of the beast, the commandment was not to have any other gods before the LORD GOD, not to make an image of anything, and not to bow down to the image or to serve it (ref. Exodus 20:3-4). The rejection of God's direct commandment is, in essence, a rejection of God Himself. God is not separate from His Word. His Word shows who He is, how He thinks, and what He expects from mankind. There is no mystery about where His heart is. It is contained in His Word. When a person refuses to obey what God has shared as important to Him, it is an outright rejection of Him.

But the result of that rejection does not occur over time. In fact, we see from the text that the aftermath of the disobedience without repentance is immediate. One hint suggesting that is a coordinating conjunction (י) in Hebrew between Genesis 3:6 and 3:7. Translated into English, that same conjunction can mean "and," "then," or "now," depending on the context of the sentence. No matter the meaning, it suggests that it was a continual action from what occurred previously.

We know in verse 6 that the woman ate the fruit and gave it to her husband to eat. In verse 7, it was not until the man ate the fruit that both their eyes were opened. Instead of operating in a spiritual view of the world around them, now Adam and Eve were painfully aware of the physical nature and limitations of their world. The full weight of that realization came with the knowledge that they were without clothes.

God was trying to keep man and woman from this knowledge so they could continue to operate without limits and boundaries under His loving, watchful eye. He knows what is best for us and tries to keep us from those things that will cause us long-term pain. But when we fail to trust Him and obey His counsel, we open ourselves to the consequences of our disobedience. This happened with the Garden of Eden, and it will happen with the mark of the beast. In the Garden of Eden, God was trying to keep man from experiencing the problems of physical and spiritual death that would come with the introduction of sin.

So what is the Word of God's warning about the mark of the beast? It is the anguish of eternal separation from God. Just like the impact of eating the forbidden fruit was instantaneous, those who accept the mark of the beast will seal their decision the instant they receive that mark on their right hand or forehead. Do not be fooled! It will not be just a visible sign of allegiance to Satan. The person's heart, thinking, and actions will be altered forever, and they will no longer be the same person they were before the mark.

No Limits/No Restrictions – I Can Do What I Want

> *For you, brethren, have been called to liberty; only do not use liberty as an opportunity for the flesh, but through love serve one another.* (Gal. 5:13, NKJV)

Liberty. Freedom. These words conjure up all kinds of thoughts in our minds. I can do whatever I want. I can say whatever I want. No one can stop me from operating in complete abandon. I don't have to consider anyone else's feelings or how my decisions may influence someone else. All of us crave the power of operating in complete freedom, but few of us will actually experience it. Liberty and freedom look different depending upon who is offering it to us. While it may look appealing from the outside, operating in liberty comes with a cost. Like so many things in this life, we get nothing for free. It will either impact us or those influenced by our decisions. But even considering the cost, the thought of being able to do whatever we want is attractive. It gives us the feeling of power and being in control.

We were created to operate in authority and have dominion over things. Leadership is an innate characteristic within many people, and there are degrees of operating in authority. Some people do not acknowledge that part of their personality or are even afraid of it; as such, it is not developed. Others realize they have an affinity for being in charge but know how to temper it and use it only when necessary. On the far end of the authority spectrum are those who crave the freedom to do whatever they want, how they want, in whatever manner they want to. The very thought of not having to answer to anyone or have any limits on what to do is a powerful attraction to most people.

For those on the extreme end of the personality spectrum, being free for whatever they want taps into deep-seated feelings of being in control. Such people, undergirded by the wrong motives and operating under evil influences, will be a formidable force to deal with. They will take shortcuts, undermine others, lie, steal, cheat, or kill to obtain and hang onto the freedom to be in control.

During the period of the mark of the beast, the Antichrist and his followers will have free reign upon the earth. As such, these people will control political, social, cultural, and economic systems all over the world. People who are not part of their group will be seen as enemies. In their social network, those who worship the Antichrist will believe they are within their rights to do anything humanly imaginable to those who don't subscribe to the doctrine of the Antichrist (i.e., Christians). The person who identifies as a Christian during this time will be killed for their testimony of Christ. Revelation 6:9-11 (NKJV) confirms this:

> *When He opened the fifth seal, I saw under the altar the souls of those who had been slain for the word of God and for the testimony which they held.* [10] *And they cried with a loud voice, saying, "How long, O LORD, holy and true, until You judge and avenge our blood on those who dwell on the earth?"* [11] *Then a white robe was given to each of them; and it was said to each of them that they should rest a little while longer, until both the number of their fellow servants and their brethren who would be killed as they were, was completed.*

Christians will be murdered because belief in Christ is a direct opposition to followers of the Antichrist. As such, those who follow the Antichrist will feel justified and even obligated by law to kill and present Christians to be killed.

False Freedom in Sin

> *Therefore do not let sin reign in your mortal body, that you should obey it in its lusts.* [13] *And do not present your members as instruments of unrighteousness to sin, but present yourselves to God as being alive from the dead, and your members as instruments of righteousness to God. For sin shall not have dominion over you, for you are not under the law but under grace.* (Rom. 6:12-14, NKJV)

We previously discussed that those who follow the Antichrist during the tribulation period will operate in a freedom fueled by the satanic world system—a system where anything goes. Any perversion or depravity that an evil human mind can invent will be allowed to flourish and manifest. Morality, ethics, and human respect for life and living will no longer exist. Sin, in all its forms, will be allowed to operate to its full capacity. Christian self-discipline and restraint will be seen as foreign and a barrier to the false freedom of sin that will be displayed. By biblical standards, sin is considered anything (thought or deed) in opposition to God's commandments. In other words, one who operates in sin chooses not to listen or obey God. Even partial obedience to God's commands is considered disobedience and, thus, sinful (1 Sam. 15:22).

Followers of the Antichrist will worship and follow him as their god. They will believe that operating to the fullness of their sin nature is the right way to live. Their bodies, minds, souls, and spirits have been contaminated by their acceptance of the mark of the beast. As such, they have made a conscious choice to renounce Jesus Christ as the LORD of their lives and have chosen to adopt Satan's false belief system. They also experience the consequences of their choice.

While they may have a false sense of freedom for a short period, they also forfeit the freedom of an eternal relationship with God. In essence, they make the crucial mistake we all make—accepting short-term pleasure in exchange for long-term consequences. The pleasures experienced may gratify the flesh in whatever perverted form that may take. Scripture reminds us that from a carnal perspective, the "flesh desires no good thing" (ref. Rom. 7:18a). As such, an individual's decisions may bring disease, emotional/psychological/social/physical trauma, or cause relationship violations between the person, other people, and ultimately God.

CHAPTER FOUR

We Must Make a Decision

The Changing Landscape of Christianity

> *For I consider that the sufferings of this present time are not worthy to be compared with the glory which shall be revealed in us.* (Rom. 8:18, NKJV)
>
> [21] *For to this you were called, because Christ also suffered for us, leaving us an example, that you should follow His steps:* [22] *"Who committed no sin, Nor was deceit found in His mouth,"* [23] *who, when He was reviled, did not revile in return; when He suffered, He did not threaten, but committed Himself to Him who judges righteously;* [24] *who Himself bore our sins in His own body on the tree, that we, having died to sins, might live for righteousness by whose stripes you were healed.* (1 Pet. 2:21-24, NKJV)

We are living in a time when it is becoming increasingly unpopular to be identified as Christian. This is a far cry from times past, when the Christian faith was seen as something to be admired and a goal to strive toward. In a 2019 study done by the Pew Research Center, researchers found that there indeed has been a decline in those who identify as Christian.

> In telephone surveys that were done in 2018 and 2019, 65% of American adults describe themselves as Christians when asked about their religion, down 12 percentage points over the past decade. Meanwhile, the religiously unaffiliated share of the population, consisting of people who describe their religious

identity as atheist, agnostic, or 'nothing in particular,' now stands at 26 percent, up from 17 percent in 2009. [9]

In the United States (U.S.), we enjoy substantial religious freedoms. Our nation was founded on Christian principles and ethical guidelines. By contrast, in Muslim nations and state-run nations, Christianity is seen as an enemy of uniformity and government control. Even in the U.S., some groups want society to be tolerant of behaviors that are contrary to biblical doctrine. So what does this perspective mean for the Christian today?

Jesus warned us in Matthew Chapter 24 that a time would come when the Christian faith would cause separation between us and other people and cause them to betray us. We will be hated for being followers of Jesus Christ. This should come as no surprise. Christians were hated in the time of Jesus because his teachings were revolutionary and opposed what the Pharisees, Sadducees, and scribes preached. When the people heard His teachings and saw His miracles, they left synagogues in droves and followed the true God.

Additionally, Christians refused to follow the pagan idols and worship styles mandated by Rome and the other nations that surrounded Jerusalem. As such, Christians were seen as threats to the status quo and had to be eliminated by whatever means necessary. Usually, that meant imprisonment, torture for individuals and their families, or even death by crucifixion, stoning, or some other method.

If we apply this mindset to modern society, it tells us that if Christianity is seen as a barrier to what society wants to do, then Christians must be eliminated. Let's draw some comparisons between how seeds of division were created against European Jews during WWII and how they compare with what Christians can expect as we progress further into the end times (see Table B below).

---

[9]   Pew Research Center, "In U.S., Decline of Christianity Continues at Rapid Pace: An Update on America's Changing Religious Landscape," 2019.

Table B – Comparison between European Jews during WWII and Christians
Subtopic: Indoctrination of Hatred

Category	European Jews During WWII	Christians
Political	Jews were seen as the cause of Germany's economic decline and inability to become a world power during the early twentieth century.	Christian morals are seen as a barrier to cultural and sexual freedom. In the end times, there will be a blend between culture, religion, and politics.
Identification	Jews, political activists, and other groups were required to wear triangles, stars, and other symbols that identified their ethnic group, political affiliation, and sexual orientation. Orthodox Jews were identified by their form of dress, cultural rituals, and religious practices.	Christians are identified by their adherence to biblical guidelines of behavior. Some denominations do have a particular form of address that distinguishes them (e.g., apostolic, some Pentecostal groups, etc.) As we get closer to the time of Christ's return, Christians who come to Christ after the Rapture of the Church will be identified by not having the mark of the beast.
Religious	Rituals such as the Passover Seder, circumcision, and bar/bat mitzvah ceremonies, strict adherence to Torah.	Rituals such as celebrations around Christmas, Christ's Resurrection, church attendance, and adherence to biblical guidelines will identify Christians as being different from society.
Social	Orthodox Jews contain their social activities within their community. Unorthodox Jews may mingle with Germans. In fact, there was some intermarriage between the two groups. During WWII, many unorthodox Jews did not identify as Jewish. They saw themselves as fully integrated with German society. It was a shock when their ethnicity labeled them as Jewish when they did not consider themselves as devout or actively practicing the faith.	Christians are basically integrated in culture. It is their faith that governs their behavior within society. The level of one's identification as Christian depends on the person's relationship with Jesus Christ and their personal adherence to biblical teachings.
Psychological	The psychological piece is the most sinister part of the indoctrination process. Here is where one idea is overlaid with the new idea that has been adopted. This can either be positive or negative. In this case, laws, propaganda, and other techniques were used to portray Jews as inferior to Germans and the reason for the decline of the economy.	Although there is no evidence yet, my opinion is that a similar process will be in operation as we progress further into the end times. Society will be fed a series of lies to suggest that Christians are not positive influences but are actually enemies of society. People will believe that by turning in Christians to be imprisoned, tortured, or killed they will be doing a public service.

One may say that this type of world will never exist and that civilized society will never allow the rounding up and killing of Christians. That is naïve thinking! Some in Nazi Germany felt the same way about its Jewish citizens until the reality could not be ignored. The persecution of Christians has been in place in some parts of the world since the first century. Even today, Christians in countries such as Africa, Iran, Turkey, Korea, China, and the Philippines face imprisonment and even death for their beliefs. Those who worship Jesus Christ in those countries do so in underground churches, cell groups, and secret meetings. Openly identifying as Christian means losing jobs, families, and livelihoods. The question is not whether the climate for Christianity is changing but how well Christians will be able to withstand the coming changes.

In the West, we have not had to deal with the trials of suffering for our faith. Because we were once a nation that stood for and demonstrated Christian ideals and principles, God had His hand of protection over us. Scripture tells us that as long as people are obedient to His commands, then those same people get access to God's blessings (ref. Deut. 28:1-2). Now that we have compromised our integrity and God's standards, we have stepped outside of God's will. As a result, God is no longer under any obligation to protect or bless us.

The Power of Choice

> *"And if it seems evil to you to serve the LORD, choose for yourselves this day whom you will serve, whether the gods which your fathers served that were on the other side of the River, or the gods of the Amorites, in the land you dwell. But as for me and my house, we will serve the LORD."* (Jos. 24:15, NKJV)

God is our Creator. He has an intrinsic knowledge of all facets of how human beings are made. He has given us a part of His divine nature. Unlike any other being God created, we can reason on an extremely high level. God has given mankind the ability to process information logically and make decisions. We make decisions every day. What to put on? What to eat? What to buy? What activities we will engage in? What to believe or not to believe?

Jesus Christ does not force us to believe in Him or have a relationship with Him. He presents the facts about who He is, what He can do, and why He wants to have a relationship with you and me. Then Jesus allows us to analyze what He has presented and allows us to make a choice about those facts. He desires that we have a relationship with Him. He created us for that purpose. But Jesus only wants a relationship with those who honestly desire a relationship with Him. He does that in the following ways: (1) Jesus presents the facts about His personality, nature, and character; (2) He tells us how much He loves us; (3) He gives us the terms and conditions regarding a relationship with Him; (4) and He shares the benefits of a long-lasting relationship with Him. He does not force us. He does not compel us. He allows us to choose.

A similar premise operates if we choose not to have a relationship with Him. Those who reject Christ in favor of Satan only do so because they are presented with partial information. We see this clearly in Genesis chapter

3 regarding Adam and Eve's decision to eat of the Tree of the Knowledge of Good and Evil. The part presented seems plausible and true. But as is characteristic for Satan, he distorts the truth and leaves out key portions that have serious implications for those who believe the lie. In this case, Satan omits the fact that by eating the fruit, Eve would lose her spiritual connection to God, open the door to her carnal nature, introduce shame and guilt into her way of thinking, and begin to suffer the pangs of physical death (Gen. 3:6-24).

This omission of the truth does not change as it relates to the mark of the beast. Accepting the mark means accepting an eternity in hell without God (Rev. 19:20), even though the False Prophet will use extreme pressure to force people to take the mark. The ultimate decision lies with the person. People must make a "yes" or "no" affirmation of where they will align themselves. But the force imposed will certainly be compelling. There will be societal, peer, economic, psychological, and religious pressure. But the most challenging form of pressure exerted will be the physical threat that may or may not lead to death.

Most humans value the sanctity of life, and the threat of death is a powerful deterrent. Some will accept the mark simply because they do not want to suffer. Others will accept it because they are afraid of dying. Scripture reminds us time after time that if the dictates of society go against the dictates of our faith, we must operate on the commands of our faith. It may mean that we have to pay for our allegiance to Christ with our lives. For the believer, physical death is not our end. In fact, it is the gateway into our eternal promises and the assurance of living with Christ forever (ref. 1 Thess. 4:13-18; 2 Cor. 5:6-10; Rom. 8:11-13; Rom. 10:9-10; and 1 John 5:10-12).

Breaking Under Pressure

> [35] *Who shall separate us from the love of Christ? Shall tribulation, or distress, or persecution, or famine, or nakedness, or peril, or sword?* [36] *As it is written: "For Your sake we are killed all day long; We are accounted as sheep for the slaughter.* [37] *Yet in all these things we are more than conquerors through Him who loved us.* [38] *For I am persuaded that neither death nor life, nor angels nor principalities nor powers, nor things present nor things to come,* [39] *nor height nor depth, nor any other created thing, shall be able to separate us from the love of God which is in Christ Jesus our LORD.* (Rom. 8:35-39, NKJV)

35 Women received their dead raised to life again. Others were tortured, not accepting deliverance, that they might obtain a better resurrection. 36 Still others had trial of mockings and scourgings, yes, and of chains and imprisonment. 37 They were stoned, they were sawn in two, were tempted, were slain with the sword. They wandered about in sheepskins and goatskins, being destitute, afflicted, tormented- 38 of whom the world was not worthy. They wandered in deserts and mountains, in dens and caves of the earth. 39 And all these, having obtained a good testimony through faith, did not receive the promise, 40 God having provided something better for us, that they should not be made perfect apart from us. (Heb. 11:35-40, NKJV)

Everything has a limit. It is the point by which something is full, has reached its maximum, and cannot go on any longer. Whether or not we want to be honest with ourselves, even Christians have a "bending point." It is the point where we wonder how we are in the situation and if the LORD is able to deliver us from it. I use the term "bending point" instead of "breaking point" because whether we "break" is totally dependent on us.

Those who can recall what we know about God, what we have experienced with God, and can elevate our focus from our situation to what the Word says about our trial can refocus, rebound, and gather enough strength to push through. By contrast, those who cannot shake themselves out of their reality and elevate their minds on spiritual matters are stuck. They begin to sink into doubt, fear, depression, and despair and become vulnerable because their mind has shifted. Instead of believing that God can and will help them, they think God is unwilling and incapable of helping. When they reach this point, they become easy prey for the enemy.

In fact, when we have doubt, we create a barrier that God cannot get through unless we remove it. Hebrews 11:6 (NKJV) tells us, *"But without faith it is impossible to please Him: for He who comes to God must believe that He is, and that He is a rewarder of them that diligently seek Him."* If we break the verse apart, it tells us that we cannot do anything to please God or make Him attentive to us unless we operate in faith. Second, we must come to Him believing He is everything that the Word and our experience tell us He is.

Finally, if we operate in faith, He rewards us for seeking Him. This "seeking" that the writer talks about is relentless. It does not give up. It perseveres despite every obstacle that comes against it. So what kind of faith do we have? We may think we have strong faith, but at some point, the very foundations of our faith will be shaken. We may then find we don't have the faith we thought we had.

Let's look at things this way: "Gold is a precious metal because of its purity. When heated at extremely high temperatures, it can be molded and crafted into any design. In certain instances, it can be beaten to the point of being transparent. The way that this is done is when the impurities that rise to the top during the melting process are scraped off and what remains is the purest form of gold." [10]

The same type of process occurs with human beings. The true nature of a person is revealed during times of trial. God allows everyone to go through periods of trial (see 1 Pet. 2:21-23; 1 Pet. 5:10-11; and James 1:2-4). No one, including Christians, is immune from going through times of pressure (John 16:33). Spiritually mature Christians have the fortitude of the Holy Spirit and the recall of the Word of God to help get them through tough times. The Holy Spirit is the Helper who aids believers during challenging times. He gives believers strength they do not have on their own. He gives them the power and confidence they need in remembering God's ability and promises that help them not break under intense pressure (Heb. 11:1). Believers know and understand that trials (even to the point of death) are not designed to break them, but they are an opportunity for God's glory to be revealed. God knows how much a person can stand. He will not allow any of His children to suffer more than they can withstand (1 Cor. 10:13).

The sad reality of many Christians is that they have not been focused on developing their spiritual life. Like the unsaved, many have gotten caught up in the cares of life—getting noticed at jobs, social circles, and in their communities. For many, a relationship with God is not their first priority but comes after everything else. We do not pray. We do not have time for individual meditation or prayer. We do not fellowship with other believers to gain insight, clarity, and understanding. We do not read our Bibles regularly.

As a result of all these things, we don't understand His commandments and do not have intimate knowledge of the LORD. The things we neglect cause us to be spiritually weak and mentally vulnerable. In this reality, we do not really know God and, thus, do not trust Him like we should. When

---

[10]   Wikipedia, "Gold," 2019, https://en.wikipedia.org/wiki/Gold.

trials come, we do not have a foundation of faith in God or His Word, so we break under pressure.

Let me make it plain! The time of the mark of the beast will be a time that has never been witnessed before in human history. Events like the Russian pogroms, the Rwandan genocide, or even the Holocaust will pale in comparison to the carnage and cruelty that will exist at this time. People alive during this period will have to make life and death decisions based on whether they will take the mark or not.

For instance, imagine parents with a sick baby who realize they cannot get medicine or medical care for their child without taking the mark. Like most caring parents, they do not want to see their child suffer. They know the consequences from an intellectual perspective, but like a lot of us, they think their experience will be different. They think God will give them a "pass" in taking the mark. They think their right-now situation outweighs what will happen in the future. So they compromise what they know, give into the emotion of the situation, and take the mark. Their emotional decision has now caused them eternal consequences—an eternity without God.

Satan's Hidden Agenda

> *"....He was a murderer from the beginning, and does not stand in the truth, because there is no truth in him. When he speaks a lie, he speaks from his own resources, for he is a liar and the father of it."*
> (John 8:44)

The one thing that Satan never tells anyone is that there is a cost for believing his lies. He always presents his lie dressed up as something wonderful. He never gives the entire story behind it. Because he has studied mankind well, he presents his lies in a way that appeals to our vanity. We must realize that whenever Satan or his cohorts presents something to us, it is always something that disobeys God's commandments and causes separation between man and God. It was his mode of operation in the Garden of Eden and has always been the case throughout human history. If history is a good indicator of past performance, then it stands to reason that his methods will not change during the great tribulation period either.

As we have learned, the mark of the beast is a symbol of mankind's decision to fully align with Satan and his agents. The person who accepts the mark has completely rejected Christ and His gift of eternal salvation. Christ has warned, prompted, and pleaded from the Scriptures throughout the ages to heed His warnings. He has given mankind ample time to repent and turn to Him. He has even delayed the outpouring of judgment to allow all who have a desire to give their lives to Him the opportunity to do so. But when the fullness of time has been reached, the LORD will carry out His plan of judgment.

Revelation chapter 14 outlines the LORD's last-ditch effort to warn mankind about the judgments about to fall upon the earth. He dispatches a series of angels to preach the gospel and give messages about what will occur. The third angel gives a specific warning regarding those who *"worship the beast and his image, and receive his mark in his forehead or in his hand"* (ref. Rev. 14:9). This angel warns that those who pledge allegiance to the beast by receiving his mark shall experience the fullness of God's wrath, which includes the following: *"He shall be tormented with fire and brimstone in the presence of the holy angels, and in the presence of the Lamb. And the smoke of their torment will go up forever; and they shall have no rest day or night"* (Rev. 14:10-11).

During the Great Tribulation, the LORD will pour out judgments in a sequence of three series of seven judgments. The first series is the seal judgments (Rev. 6:1-8:5). The second series is the trumpet judgments (Rev. 8:6-14:20). The final series is the vial or bowl judgments (Rev. 15:1-18:24). The description of the bowl judgments is outlined in great detail in Revelation chapter 16. These are reserved for those inhabitants of the earth who have made a conscious decision to reject Christ. Each series of judgments increase in intensity as each new one is poured out. The vial/bowl judgments contain the fullness of God's wrath that will be released. The table below outlines in detail what will occur during the time of the vial/bowl judgments (see Table C below).

Table C – Detailed Account of the Vial/Bowl Judgments

Judgment	Scripture Reference
"Foul and loathsome sores" that come upon those who have the mark of the beast and those who worship his image.	Revelation 16:1-2
The sea becomes as blood and every living sea creature dies.	Revelation 16:3
The rivers and springs of water become blood.	Revelation 16:4-7
The sun scorches men with fire and great heat.	Revelation 16:8
The kingdom of the beast becomes full of darkness and its followers will gnaw their tongues because of the pain of the sores. NOTE: Those who have the mark of the beast blaspheme God because of their pains and sores and do not repent of their deeds.	Revelation 16:10-11
The Euphrates River dries up so that it will become the path by which those who aligned with Satan and his agents will fight the LORD and his army at the Battle of Armageddon. Demonic spirits will stir up the kings of the earth and the whole world will engage in battle with the LORD Jesus Christ.	Revelation 16:12-16
Great lightning, thunder, and a great earthquake will occur on the earth. The earthquake is unlike any that has occurred before. The great city (Babylon) will be divided into three pieces and the cities of the nations will fall. God will pour out the fullness of His wrath on Babylon. The islands and mountains will go away in the destruction of the earth.	Revelation 16:19-20
A great hailstorm will fall upon the earth. The hail will be huge pellets that will equate to 1 talent or 100 lbs. each.	Revelation 16:21

Believe it or not, there is no turning back once a person receives the mark of the beast. The person's mind, heart, soul, and spirit become seared, and their consciousness altered upon receipt. There is no do-over or "I did not mean to do it" because they utterly refused to surrender, repent, and allow Jesus Christ to save their souls. As a result, their names are not written in the Lamb's Book of Life and they are sentenced to burn in the lake of fire to be eternally separated from God, **FOREVER!** (Rev. 20:15).

We Need God!

"For God so loved the world that He gave His only begotten Son, that whoever believes in Him should not perish but have everlasting life." (John 3:16, NKJV)

Jesus said to him, "I am the way, the truth, and the life. No one comes to the Father except through Me." (John 14:6, NKJV)

Ultimately, we live and function because of God. Without Him, we are nothing and have nothing. This is a hard concept for many people to accept. We have been conditioned to think we have either success or failure because of our intelligence and efforts alone. In reality, our failures and successes are determined by whether we submit our desires to God and align ourselves with His plan for our lives.

Our pride is our greatest barrier to finding true happiness. Scripture tells us that if we continue in pride, we chart the course for our eventual destruction (Prov. 16:18). Pride creates a barrier between us, God, and other people. It gives us a narrow focus and makes us believe we don't need anyone else. Whatever we need or whatever we have to get, we can do it by ourselves and by our own means. Our pride makes it hard to admit that we need help and do not have all the answers to our questions. Our pride makes it hard to admit that despite whatever fragments of happiness and contentment we can scrape together, we are still restless and unfulfilled. Our pride makes it hard to admit that **We Need God!**

Some people will read this book who do not believe in God. They do not believe He even exists. My question for them is, "How did you get here?" Most people would say through the procreative unity of their parents. Some would argue through evolution—the belief that "all of life, including man, has been derived from lower forms. There have been mutation changes so that new life forms have developed."[11] Another view called "Theistic Evolution" suggests that "God controlled the whole mechanism of the evolutionary process to bring about the universe as we know it. He used evolution to bring the world into being. Man came through the brute beasts. This view is used assimilate philosophy, modern scientific theory, and the Bible."[12]

---

[11] Grudem, *Systematic Theology,* 279-280.
[12] Meyer, "Defining Theistic Evolution: An Introduction to the Book *Theistic Evolution: A Scientific, Philosophical, and Theological Critique.*" Theistic Evolution (February 2019): 8. https://www.discovery.org/a/defining-theistic-evolution/.

One must remember that for any type of evolutionary theory to be valid, the species must have an origin or beginning point. So where did the beginning begin? Archaeological and scientific data constantly refutes the evolution argument because of the inability to adequately answer this question.

This is where the Bible comes in and answers the question of the origin of the beginning. The answer is housed in the first few lines of the book of Genesis: [1] *In the beginning God created the heavens and the earth.* [2] *The earth was without form and void; and darkness was on the face of the deep. And the Spirit of God was hovering over the face of the waters.* [3] *Then God said, "Let there be light" and there was light* (Gen. 1:1-3, NKJV). Before anything existed, God was already there. Until He spoke light into being, nothing else could be created. God's speaking set the precedent for the earth's environment to be created, then the earth, and then the living things that would inhabit the earth (Gen. 1:4-25). The final thing God created was man and woman (Gen. 1:26-27).

Mankind was different than any other being God created. In mankind, God put His image and His likeness. He also created man and woman to be productive and multiply God's likeness and image upon the earth. Additionally, they are to replenish, subdue, and have dominion over every living thing God created (Gen. 1:27-29). God put His Spirit inside of man, and with it, He gave him the ability to speak, think logically, and have wisdom and knowledge. God taught man that his ability to speak would cause things to be named according to that which was spoken. With the gift of speech, man would have the ability to assign a name, identity, and function to that which he named (Gen. 2:19-20).

The most important function for man was that he was not just to be a created being. God created mankind to have an intimate relationship with Him. When God put His Spirit (pneuma) inside of mankind, He put a piece of Himself within them and is now personally invested in His creation. His Holy Spirit became the seal that connected man to God. When we sin, we feel darkness and isolation because the connection is broken. The only way to reestablish the connection is to honestly confess our sin and accept and believe in Jesus Christ as our LORD and Savior. Then and only then can we be restored to fellowship with God.

Until we reconcile ourselves back to God, we *will never* be whole. We will always try to find something or someone to fill the emptiness. The other things we get into may work for a short while, but we will always need more and more of whatever "it" is to get the feeling of being filled.

Depending on what "it" is and the more we get of "it," "it" may do us more harm than good.

If "it" is drugs, sex, alcohol, or some other vice, the more we get, the more we will get addicted to "it" and how "it" makes us feel. As we continue, we will get into a much worse state than when we started. We will still be inwardly empty, and our lives will be a trail of wasted years, broken relationships, shattered promises, and damage. Only having a personal relationship with Jesus Christ will heal the emptiness in our soul on a permanent basis. All we have to do is quit using substitutes and just allow Him to come into our lives and give us the wholeness and happiness we desperately crave.

When the mark of the beast is presented, everything will be so corrupted that many will have no idea what to believe. The lies will be presented as truth, and truth will be seen as lies. To the one reading this book, I am telling you right now.....**Do Not Accept The Mark!** You will be condemning yourself and those around you (by association) to eternal separation from God. I know it may be difficult to say **no,** and many things around you might pressure you into saying **yes.** I beg you not to listen; there is another way.

Do not allow fear, pride, or anything else to keep you from the full life you can have in Jesus Christ. You do not have to live the rest of your life chasing one high after another, trying to fill the hole in your heart and your soul. Today, all you have to do is lay aside the weight of your struggle, humble yourself, and admit that you need God right now.....Today!

Jesus Christ says in John 10:10 (NKJV): "The thief does not come except to steal, and to kill, and to destroy. I have come that they might have life, and that they may have it more abundantly." The "thief" here is Satan. He does not want you to have freedom and wants you to destroy your life. He does everything he can to keep you under the cover of deception. Why? He wants as much company in hell as He can get. He knows that his time is short, and he is trying to do as much damage as he can to get people to choose to take the mark.

Jesus does not want anyone to go to hell. Hell is a prepared place for a prepared people. Those who end up there do so by personal choice because Jesus and the Scriptures have disclosed how to avoid it. Jesus loves us and gave His life for everyone on the cross so that no one will have to go there. All we have to do is accept His gift of salvation. It is the choice of each person to accept that free gift.

Invitation to Discipleship

If you are reading this book and do not know how to go about receiving Jesus as your personal Savior, you can pray this simple prayer:

> *Jesus, please help me! I don't know what to say, and I don't know how to pray. All I know is that I need my life to change. I believe in my heart that you love me. You love me so much that you died on the cross for my sins. I believe that God raised you from the dead and that now you sit in heaven on His right hand. Please forgive me for my sins, and I accept you as LORD over my life. In your name, Jesus, I pray. Amen.*

If you have accepted Jesus Christ as your personal Savior, I would like to hear from you and pray for you as you progress on your Christian journey. I would like to connect you with local places of worship in your area that can help grow you into an effective disciple of Jesus Christ.

You can reach me at:
Email: wordcarrier6901@yahoo.com
Email #2: pastorkarenphillips@gmail.com
Facebook: www.facebook.com/karen.phillips

Blessings to you, and Welcome to the Family of God!!

Bibliography

Brand, Chad, Charles Draper, and Archie England, eds. 2003. *Holman Illustrated Bible Dictionary*. Nashville: Holman Bible Publishers.

Bullinger, E.W. 1967. *The Number in Scripture: Its Supernatural Design and Spiritual Significance*. Grand Rapids: Kregel Publications.

Grudem, Wayne. 1994. *Systematic Theology: An Introduction to Biblical Doctrine*. Grand Rapids: Zondervan.

Merriam Webster's Dictionary and Thesaurus. 2006. Springfield: Merriam-Webster, Incorporated.

Meyer, Stephen. 2019. "Defining Theistic Evolution: An Introduction to the Book *Theistic Evolution: A Scientific, Philosophical, and Theological Critique.*" *Theistic Evolution* (February): 1-30. https://www.discovery.org/a/defining-theistic-evolution/.

Pew Research Center. 2019. "In U.S., Decline of Christianity Continues at Rapid Pace: An Update on America's Changing Religious Landscape." https://www.pewforum.org/2019/10/17/in-u-s-decline-of-christianity-continues-at-rapid-pace.

Sax, Benjamin and Dieter Kuntz. 1992. *Inside Hitler's Germany: A Documentary History of Life in the Third Reich*. Lexington: D.C. Heath and Company.

Wikipedia. "Gold." https://en.wikipedia.org/wiki/Gold. Accessed 03/02/2021

Willard, Dallas and Don Simpson. 2005. *Revolution of Character: Discovering Christ's Pattern for Spiritual Transformation.* Colorado Springs: Nav. Press.

Acknowledgments

I want to thank my husband, Rodney Phillips, and our children (Brittani, Jaylen, and Shayla) for your constant encouragement as I was writing this book. All of you were my first critics and constant supporters. I appreciate your candor and patience as I picked your brains for honest feedback. When I needed you to push me, you told me to keep going.

Now the book is finished! Thank you for your faith in Our God to help me and your faith in me that I could do it. I love you all!

About the Author

Karen P. Phillips, MDiv, serves as one of the pastors at Christ Central Ministries in Columbia, South Carolina. She has broad experience and expertise in strategic partnership engagement, Christian education program development, and ministry leadership training and development.

She is a sought-after preacher, teacher, and conference speaker. Karen is a student at Columbia International University, where she is pursuing a Doctoral degree in ministry leadership. Currently, she is working on her second book.

Her greatest joy is living her life as a wife to her husband, Rodney Phillips, and mother to her children: Brittani, Jaylen, and Shayla.

CPSIA information can be obtained
at www.ICGtesting.com
Printed in the USA
BVHW030956310821
615687BV00012B/299